ELPIS' ECSTASY
Hope as Home

PRISHA GOEL

BLUEROSE PUBLISHERS
India | U.K.

Copyright © Prisha Goel 2025

All rights reserved by author. No part of this publication may be reproduced, stored in a retrieval system or transmitted in any form or by any means, electronic, mechanical, photocopying, recording or otherwise, without the prior permission of the author. Although every precaution has been taken to verify the accuracy of the information contained herein, the publisher assumes no responsibility for any errors or omissions. No liability is assumed for damages that may result from the use of information contained within.

BlueRose Publishers takes no responsibility for any damages, losses, or liabilities that may arise from the use or misuse of the information, products, or services provided in this publication.

For permissions requests or inquiries regarding this publication, please contact:

BLUEROSE PUBLISHERS
www.BlueRoseONE.com
info@bluerosepublishers.com
+91 8882 898 898
+4407342408967

ISBN: 978-93-6783-298-1

Cover design: Daksh
Typesetting: Tanya Raj Upadhyay

First Edition: May 2025

For all those who love the night

but find light amidst the darkness.

Acknowledgements

To the woman who sparked the love I share for poetry, Mumma, thank you. You have seen through my every mask and still chose to stand by me through it all. I couldn't have asked for a better source of my existence.

To the man who made it all possible, Papa, thank you. I know no matter where I am, you'll always have my back.

To my family and friends, thank you for shaping me through shared experiences, for your encouragement and belief in me.

To my teachers and mentors, I can't thank you enough for supporting my every venture and loving me endlessly. Whether it be through your words, or by helping me explore new versions of myself or by cherishing my growth and growing with me, you have impacted me in ways I can't describe.

To my readers, thank you for trusting me enough to pick up this book. I hope to foster an everlasting connection with you as we begin this journey together.

To the little girl in me, thank you for always dreaming big and sharing your smile with me. I owe it all to you.

Preface

Thoughts flood my mind. Flood seems like a negative word here, but navigating through all these thoughts can prove to be challenging.

I have come to a realisation over time- I am sensitive- I feel things deeply and I have embraced this about myself. It wasn't an overnight change; it took time but eventually happened. In my dealings with people, places and things, this quality often creeps in. I then find myself surrounded by a multitude of thoughts that follow and to navigate through it all, I begin to write. The journey of thoughts from my head and heart to the paper might take different paths but all lead to a similar destination. The destination of hope.

Elpis- the Goddess of Hope- symbolises this destination. The legend goes that when Pandora's curiosity overpowered her senses and she opened her jar, she released all evils into the world. As these horrors spread and plagued the world, she quickly closed the jar, trapping hope inside. This struck a chord as I drew parallels with my writing. Through all hardships, emotions and confusions, hope is always the last thing to remain.

Each poem is preceded by a related thought.

I have left a few pages blank at the end of the book and they are meant for you. Yes, you can use this space to express yourself whether it is through writing, drawing or any other form of art.

I hope you find yourself immersed in reading as I found myself immersed in writing.

Table of Contents

Clouds 3

Two Streams 5

The Street 9

Missing 11

Dilemma 15

Sensing Silences 17

Eccedentesiast 21

Sea of Life: How I see it! 23

Trusting Tangibility 27

Emptiness 29

Escalating Emotions 33

Empathy 35

Lightning 39

Twinkling Times 41

Levelling Love? 45

Questioning Quests 47

Slow down 51

Can we really catch dreams? 53

Maybe 55

New me? 59

She was given an assignment, others labelled it as a cakewalk, something easy, but she pondered like never before. It wasn't some complicated calculus or nuclear fusion but a simple question that demanded a one-word answer; she was asked to describe herself in a single word. As she thought, calculus suddenly seemed easier as she believed "To define was to limit". One word couldn't encapsulate all that she had to offer because she wanted to soar high, to be limitless- something far beyond the scope of a single answer. As she navigated through an array of these thoughts, she finally reached a conclusion: a dreamer, that's what she was!

Clouds

Big white clouds in the sky,
I want to catch them and fly.
I've seen rabbits, castles, monsters and ghosts,
I wonder what stories they behold that are waiting to be told.
I was gazing at a cloud and suddenly, it burst out raining,
Were all those stories being shattered; my heart started aching.
But when I woke up the next day, the clouds came up again smiling,
it was mystical but isn't life all about new beginnings?

The stage is set, podiums placed, as the proposition and opposition sit down to debate. The venue, you might wonder, is her brain and the debate starts at an unprecedented time, she claims. Both sides make strong arguments about the motion for the day. In this world, we often come at crossroads wherein we constantly debate over whether to align our actions with how we are treated by others or continue to stay true to ourselves. It is a debate over keeping our inner compass steady or riding the waves of reality whilst changing with them. She navigates through the feeling of perplexion as she aims to decide the ultimate winner but there seems to have been an unlikely shift in the debate, as eventually, both sides find common ground.

Two Streams

Two streams run parallel in the trajectory of my mind,
should I reciprocate energies or continue being kind?
Kindness and sensitivity give me purpose,
but shouldn't I follow "You get what you give," the thought makes me nervous.
Following is not something I've been the best at,
neither have I ever wanted to; I hear myself chat.
Energies are a reflection of the internalized state,
maybe love is what I can give to conquer that hate.
Likewise, the streams start to converge,
my calmness could counter their upsurge.
Apathy treated with my consideration,
Negativity taking a complete obliteration.
We can't control others' energies, I claim,
So, to bring light in the world irrespective of the darkness, is my aim.

We're all circling in our own bubble, often so consumed by it that we forget that ours isn't the only one. There exist billions of such bubbles, not hidden in an alternate universe but lost among the familiar. She attempts to pop her bubble of bliss and witness the magical stories that unfold all around her.

The Street

I walked down the street today,
I guess I wanted to get away.
But I forgot, what I was trying to forget,
amidst a street filled with muses, a living vignette.
I saw a little girl glaring lovingly at her mother,
they were standing outside a wedding dress store and for them, it might be a day like any other.
I start to anticipate the day they'll return, this time, stepping inside,
The little girl tries on the dress with her mother standing beside.
A realisation strikes, that day will be etched in their hearts forever, for it was not just a normal sight.
Across the street, I notice a bench,
an elderly couple sits; in love, they drench.
They hold hands, reflecting on times they've spent
knowing that for each other, they were always meant.
I move forward and see,
a young couple looking into each other's eyes, oh they seem so free.
I couldn't comprehend what this freedom meant
until I looked up at a pair of birds on a tree and this feeling, I now reinvent.
I walked down the street today,
and while I was away,
all I remembered was that this feeling, this freedom I longed for was love,
it was all around, only if we looked enough and noticed the signs from above.

Each creature that inhabits this earth has a fate of its own, a destination and journey unlike any other. However, certain paths intersect but these points of intersection aren't always the endpoints. It's math! Each of the two lines extends infinitely in both directions. But the intersection creates a concept- a funny one, but a great pursuit: missing someone. It can be experienced circling the point of intersection or reflecting on the points that lie before you.

Missing

"I miss you", I let out the weight off my chest,
Missing someone has truly been a mysterious quest.
I miss you; it took me a while to admit,
I tried to pull away but eventually, I quit.
I miss the idea of you or I miss me with you, it's hard to comprehend,
but I don't let it show, not yet, so I start to pretend.
This game of pretence leaves me drained,
I can't help myself but pick up the phone to call and immediately feel untamed.
Missing leaves you daydreaming about endless possibilities,
and you are the sole composer of all these symphonies.
Missing someone is a blessing and a curse altogether,
I long for something that might not even exist but there is still some hope to which I surrender.

There was a time some might call trying. For others, it might be just another ordinary day but for her, it could alter the course of her life or at least that's what it felt like in the moment.

At that juncture, she was given a choice she had to make. On the surface level, it wasn't that hard, but oh, the intricacies of her mind perplexed her for weighing both alternatives yielded an uncertain result: a balance that added to her conquest. A conquest of choosing between potentially losing what she had built with gentle care and hard work or losing out on a moment she had been waiting for a long time: something she was so fond of, an emotion she wanted to experience for as long as she could remember. The silent battles she fought led her to make a decision, choosing what felt right in the moment.

Dilemma

Today, I was faced with a choice,
one I didn't want to voice.
It's a tug of war in my brain,
and all it does to me is bring pain and drain.
Worrying is just in vain, I hear
but the pain I feel is no less, I fear.
So, I sit and think,
It's been hours since I now blink.
A sudden thud, a hollow clink,
"Will the ship I built sink?"
I go towards the sound and see,
the anchor isn't there and the ship is free.
I see it going away
my heart wants it to stay
but as I stand at the bay,
the ship didn't sink at least, I say.

Change is the only constant- a cliché statement to make, but she's believed in it ever since she can remember. The scope of this word transcends boundaries. It can be applied to people, places, things and most certainly, relationships. Equations can change in the blink of an eye. As she looks out the car window filled with dew, she reflects on how beautifully curated relations can also be met with silence...

Sensing Silences

The silence is loud, many words unsaid,
Even feelings that were once woven carefully seem like a fragile thread.
We're in the same room but it doesn't feel so same anymore,
as I write, why does it feel like the memories we made once, we ourselves tore?
As the page ripped, we drew apart,
now heralding comes the new start.
Usually, I'd be excited to begin something new,
but maybe that was when it was with you.
That's what is weird with change,
silences that were once comforting turned into a cage.
Hours went by, words unsaid,
because your presence was enough to get us ahead.
Your presence is still felt but not like before,
the silences remain, but for them to end, I implore.
The end is far, it seems,
then you look at me, maybe there's hope after all, oh how it gleams.

Language is exquisite. The vast pool of words it guarantees leaves even a non-swimmer finding themselves enjoying this ceaseless pool. She also found herself lost in this world as she came across a word she'd never heard before but resonated with: something that so well described a state that she saw many, including her, experience.

Eccedentesiast

Eccedentesiast, a new word I came across,
"Hiding pain behind a smile"; what a shame, what a loss.
Moments flash before my eyes when I've been a victim of this "shame"
is it all such a facade, a pointless game?
Then why do we all play,
impersonating society's puppets made of clay?
God created different emotions for a reason,
it is okay to feel them as they change like seasons.
The word is derived from Latin and translates to
someone who performs by showing teeth,
the world seems to ace the art of performing but in this act, forgets how to breathe.
But then I remember the times I've smiled at strangers,
even when my own mind was filled with its own dangers.
They smiled back displaying humanity's beautiful array,
both our smiles wielded swords to send sorrows away.

As she stands at the shore looking at the journey she has undertaken, she feels content. Sand's warm embrace and the whisper of the ocean's kisses bring with them a sense of bliss. She starts to trace parallels between the sea and life. Placing herself into the picture, she realises the role of a traveller. As she continues her voyage cruising over tides that come her way, she unravels the mysteries found in the depths of the sea.

Sea of Life: How I see it!

We're all sailing in the sea of life,
same sea yet different ships, different journeys, where we thrive.
Sometimes calm, sometimes full of high tides,
it's funny how we're all still trying to hide.
But hiding isn't the way forward,
rowing is what will get you through, coward.
'Coward', the word seems too harsh to use,
so, let's make a pact not to hide and call it a truce.
There is no right or wrong, black or white,
sometimes, grey is what gets you through life.
Not every sunshine after rain leaves behind rainbows,
it's essential to strike a balance between all your highs and lows.
Because balance is what will keep your boat from tumbling,
everything can be put together even if it feels like it's all just crumbling.
Not everything can be comprehended in terms of first, second and last,
because every star, big or small, has its own light to cast.
In this rat race to win, many ships collide,
instead of fighting, why don't we lift each other and slip aside our pride?
Because in the end, what's more important is that none of the ships sink,
or it's all going to be over in just one blink.

A vase filled with flowers is a serene sight but as she sees it falling, a string of thoughts runs through her mind. She attributes the falling of the vase to its fragility and claims that the tangibility was at fault. Certain things start to seem too tangible but the story unfolds in a context embedded within her.

Trusting Tangibility

The heart, a tangible thing
too tangible to be trusted, I presume
Two hearts, woven intricately with a string
until the string is cut bringing their doom.

Two hearts, equally tangible,
joyfully carrying each other's weight
until at one point, they stumble
then a greater barrier arrives and the fall causes them to separate.

Two hearts, tangible enough,
get tired after trying
a situation so tough that they begin to bluff
can't recover those old strings by buying.

Two hearts, longing to be tangible
to be seen and felt
until they meet someone so compatible,
the strings regenerate as the hearts are held.

Certain feelings creep in, in the most unlikely ways and places, and leave us confused with the multitude of incomprehensible thoughts of emptiness amidst a sea of faces. We all, at some point in time, long to belong. So does she. The longing creates an unexplainable void: a blank canvas filled with emotion.

Emptiness

I sit in a crowded room with loud chittering,
yet there's a void; I can't put into words what my soul is whispering.
But I feel compelled to express this emptiness
I look around, pen and paper are all I find to confide in, and hopefully achieve a sense of happiness.
So, I begin to write; my pencil quivers and it is an absolute fright
wasn't this coping mechanism, always right?
Writing is supposed to take me to a world, so bright
so why am I here feeling helpless and tight?
The questions flood my brain and to win over this chaos, I can't seem to summon the courage of a knight
I feel like everything suddenly turned white
A colour that described my plight
It is called the source of light
but for me, it embodied emptiness; the feeling I was trying so hard to fight.

Everyone experiences emotions; so does she. However, she feels, feels and continues to feel so deeply that the emotions swell within her, rising until they reach their peak. They start to overpower and seem uncontrollable and she, being a control freak, starts to become restless. She seems to find no solution but things pan out in a way that deems just right...

Escalating Emotions

Water boils on the kitchen stove,

the bubbles emerge, and tension they evoke.

The steam connects bubbles to my suppressed emotions,

their boiling point reached, the pressure too intense;

oh, should've taken precautions.

The sensations that once possessed the freedom to flow had been bottled up for long enough,

now to stop this influx and rising seemed too tough.

As the water was about to overflow,

the gas flame was brought down to a low.

How could I do this with my heart? I asked the steam,

the silence was heard but very soon it was going to be redeemed.

Suddenly, milk was poured followed by sugar and tea leaves,

oh, even the boiling water deceives.

It was tea that was coming together all along,

the steam turned to fragrant fumes as that's where it truly belonged.

The fumes now answered what steam couldn't before,

just give your heart the chance to explore.

Studies show that the human mind can experience about 60,000 thoughts every day. She believes these findings to be accurate since she encounters, what seems like, a whirlpool of notions every fleeting moment. At times, she feels it is hard to sail across all these notions herself so the mere thought of someone else being able to understand what she, herself, cannot process seems impossible to her. She concludes that no one can truly empathise with another being but as the waves of reflection wash over her, she discovers that not everything can be categorised by a mere glance.

Empathy

I heard someone say that one must be empathetic,

grappled by problems that might start to feel like a phenomenon, so magnetic.

But I wonder, how my entangled brain can be comprehended by someone,

when all these emotions, I, myself, cannot summon.

Putting yourself in someone's shoes starts to seem impossible to me,

we can never understand how deeply it hurts until we feel it, I guarantee.

As I pondered the worth of this word,

a slight whisper is what I heard.

What you're thinking is not absurd

but emotions are a concept- so vague, so blurred.

So, all we can do is try, right?

to maybe be the source of light

and help provide hope despite all the spite.

There is a natural tendency to look at certain things from a specific lens, often overlooking the beauty that lies beneath. As she looks at the sky, exhibiting its power and might, as she claims at the moment, she feels scared. The sound of thunder and the lightning terrify her but as she sees through this veil, there is a shift in her soul. It's like her heart taking a U-turn. She sees in the electric beams the portrayal of one of the most powerful emotions...

Lightning

Powerful beams struck the ground today,
and I trembled in dismay.
I associated them with fear and despair,
every fibre of my being screamed, "Beware".
I asked myself why,
is this my reflex to comply?
but just as another beam struck the ground,
it no longer made me feel as if I drowned.
This time, it was different
I didn't feel so ignorant.
The light was a symbol of the deepest of emotions
the clouds yearned to meet the ground with devotion
amidst all this commotion.
If this isn't love, what is? I thought
it is nature's bliss, the truth I caught.
Lightning is often termed as destructive and extreme,
but isn't that what love is, a powerful beam.
I begin to connect my inherent emotional sparks with those in the sky
and suddenly, the despair turned to hope and I could fly.
Love should know no bounds and so doesn't lightning,
the next time the beam struck the ground, the trembling finally turned to rising.

"Birthdays are magical", says the little girl in me, counting down the days to her birthday. Excitement surrounds her like fairy dust, sparkling all over her. As she twirls in her mystical spotlight, feeling like her favourite princess, there is a sudden shift: she is older now. Certain feelings start to creep in, and she thinks about how time is limited and the clock is ticking. Amidst all this, magic takes the front seat and steers her in a direction, which she unknowingly needed: the destination being the dreamy world for a meet-up with the little girl who is giggling and dancing, waiting for their birthday.

Twinkling Times

As I gaze upon the clock, awaiting the stroke of midnight,

each movement of its hand mirrors the flickering light.

For many what might just be another day,

it's the evidence of my existence, I say.

Filled with fear and gratitude at the same time,

then comes the clock's ticking chime.

There is a conflict within my brain,

excitement and change dance around while fear and anxiety suffer in pain.

Change moves towards fear in an attempt to communicate,

it shares the joy and the idea to celebrate.

The fear, worried about the declining future reflects on the past,

oh, the change clearly had a magic spell it cast.

I reflect on the times that have passed by,

all memories- perfect souvenirs of bygone phases stored in a place on which I could rely.

The clock strikes midnight, completing a full cycle,

from the day I was born, peddling and stopping to look around once in a while describes this beautiful journey's title.

It's in the actions, gestures, eyes and most importantly hearts: love. However the quantity or quality isn't always matched. Well, setting up these standards defeat the very purpose of this word. A thought creeps into her mind as she lets her tendency to want everything sorted get in the way of complexities that transcend order. She starts to question if she's in the wrong for loving with all her heart in a world that, at times, can seem as steady as shifting sand.

Levelling Love?

The love we give isn't always the love we receive,

You're curating fantasies while they're preparing to deceive.

"Why me?" You ask the universe,

Hoping it will somehow reimburse.

You feel deeply and loved too strong,

But why did you love someone who didn't belong?

You ask the universe, "Can no one reciprocate the love I give?"

"Will I be an overflowing cup for as long as I live?"

I can't wait for more people to drain me, I say,

Should I stop loving this way?

This is when the universe steps in,

And takes me around for a spin.

You've been created with love to love, it claims,

And to keep filling your cup is one of my greatest aims.

As I look in the mirror and see my face,

I am full of love; I begin to embrace.

I'll continue to love with all my heart,

Because I've been blessed with this beautiful art.

There are questions all around her, questions many might not even realise exist, but she seeks answers to them. The constant quest for these answers builds up in her head, but what meets the world's eyes is just plain silence. She is in search of words to transform this silence and voice her questions but she finds no soul who'd be able to answer. As the search continues, she strives harder to be given the opportunity to be heard and starts to long for it. After relentless striving comes the day- the day she had been waiting for but as the opportunity lies in front of her, looking at her dreamy eyes, she...

Questioning Quests

Answers we seek to questions untold,

there's a storm that lies within but takes too long to unfold.

The storm was preceded by a silence,

a silence filled with words that couldn't get their license.

Who would give this license, when, where, how; the questions circle around,

and the silence finds itself in a storm where the sound was found.

Was this the sound it had continued to seek,

the seeker was left in a situation so bleak.

The license which was longed for was given,

but now all the silence wanted was to listen.

She is ambitious, too ambitious for her age. A misfit: that's what she is. Society labels her and masks their labels with the decorated curtains of concern. She should slow down. She must take things easy, slow. She is too fast, they say, as they keep a check on her speed. But she knows her dreams, she is working towards her reality and the clamour she hears starts to fade as the music of her life takes over.

Slow down

"Slow down," I hear,

"Don't beat yourself up, dear"

but the cost is too high, I fear.

The consequences flood my brain, so severe they appear.

"Slow down," it's easy for others to say,

but if I'm fast, who knows the correct speed, I think as I lay.

Who decides my pace, if not me?

Have I really turned my life into a mindless spree?

"Slow down," the voice echoes louder than before,

Should I really not try to alter the timeline to get ahead, I implore.

Is it really about getting ahead, or is this my real pace?

Not everyone shares timelines as it's life, not a race.

Lying, pondering, looking at the vastness that lies above,

stars are a reminder that I create the life I love.

"Slow down," I hear again,

this time, I keep running, as the phrase seems too mundane.

As she snuggles in her bed, across it, she glances at her study table. As books and notes surround and form a daily sight, she notices what she now calls the disco ball of her library: her dream catcher. It had been there for what seemed like always but today, she can't help but keep looking at it. Had she never given it enough attention before? Had she overlooked it, labelled it as nothing more than an added aesthetic? She delves into her inner cosmos and starts to wonder how easily one can fail to see the soul beneath the surface of daily encounters.

Can we really catch dreams?

I passed a store where I saw a spectrum of dream catchers, as we call them,

can dreams really be caught in this realm?

An intricate web woven around the circle of life,

with feathers as the messengers, they give dreams flight.

As I traced the origins, a truth unveiled,

dream catchers were a source of protection, it entailed.

Mothers who were away longed to protect their children even in their sleep,

so, they crafted this beauty with love, oh so deep.

The web entangles the bad dreams, while good dreams can pass,

each adversity will ward off as the sun shines; why was this not taught in our class?

As I turn off the lights, the fear of nightmares creeps in,

I think about the realm of ceaseless possibilities, closing my eyes with nothing but a grin.

Everything is steady and sound, just as it should be. On the outlook, spotless! But an inner conflict emerges and she starts to see ripples in this symmetry. We present ourselves to the outside world in a manner that often disorients itself with the world within us. She navigates through the confusing cosmos that lies in her being, something only she has access to, yet something that feels out of control. In moments like these, even a slight glimmer, a chance, can make all the difference...

Maybe

When everything seems to be going right,
but a slight whisper from your heart is all your fright.
If it's all so fine,
why is there such a long line?
A long line to love, to be heard, to feel understood;
where did all that go, the childhood?
but isn't that what I'm supposed to be living now,
aren't these supposed to be the best years; just wow!
but here I am, feeling overwhelmed,
doing nothing yet being completely drenched.
Everything seems to be going right,
but aren't we all happy faces with internal fights?
I wonder if I will ever win,
and this thought gets under my skin.
It's all about winning, isn't it
maybe it's not, I start to wonder.
Maybe, just maybe, everything is not fine
Who is the one to define?
So with a sigh,
I say, this very moment could be my high.
Vulnerability is not weakness, maybe,
So here is my plea:

Let's all accept and embrace,

for there is nothing wrong with moving at your own pace.

It's okay to feel, to want to be loved and to be heard,

for it's our journey, and with time, it won't all feel so blurred.

Maybe it will or maybe not, but the word "maybe" just gives me hope.

everything will be fine because there is always scope.

"You've changed so much. Is it like a 'new year, new me' phase?", her friend laughingly says. She starts to think and putting things into perspective helps her realise that change surrounds her. It does: a lot has changed- both within and outside. Her friend's words circle in her mind as the idea of a 'new me' starts to bother her. She pictures the little girl in her, smiling the biggest smile, and is left to wonder if this 'new her' has left that girl behind...

New me?

Circumstances, priorities, and dreams cause you to change,
this can seem very strange.
There is a diverse range that now exists,
 confusing to navigate, through all that it consists.
Labelling it as a "new me" starts to seem like betrayal,
If I loved who I was, why this new portrayal?
If all this is new, is there no old left?
It feels like an identity theft.
The idea of a "new me" is misunderstood,
Evolving isn't the same as replacing, it's good.
I start to accept that I have changed,
I've gotten closer to my cores, not estranged.
Moving forward doesn't have to carry the guilt of neglecting the past,
So, I change proudly, and a magic spell, I cast.

www.ingramcontent.com/pod-product-compliance
Lightning Source LLC
LaVergne TN
LVHW041631070526
838199LV00052B/3312